T0088707

NOTE

This work was written for the National Federation of Women's Institutes and was given its first performance by massed choirs of the Federation at the Royal Albert Hall on June 15th, 1950.

Acknowledgements :

Thanks are due to the following for permitting the use of copyright words and/or tunes :—

Messrs. Boosey & Hawkes Ltd. :

" God Bless the Master "
from *English Traditional Songs and Ballads*
edited by L. E. Broadwood.

Messrs. Cramer & Co., Ltd. (London):

" In Bethlehem City "
and " May Day Song " (2nd tune)
from *English County Songs*.

Messrs. Novello & Co., Ltd. :

" The Lark in the Morning "
" The Cuckoo "
" Sheep Shearing "
" John Barleycorn "
" The Unquiet Grave "

The purchase or hire of this work does not convey the right to perform, for which permission in the United Kingdom must be obtained from the Performing Right Society Limited.

The Vocal Score is published separately

Orchestral material is available on hire

FOLK SONGS OF THE FOUR SEASONS

A Cantata for Women's Voices

with Orchestral or Pianoforte accompaniment

R. VAUGHAN WILLIAMS

Voice Parts

OXFORD UNIVERSITY PRESS

PROLOGUE

TO THE PLOUGHBOY

(For All Voices with Semi-chorus Descant)

Folk-song

Arranged by
R. VAUGHAN WILLIAMS

Copyright, 1950, by the Oxford University Press, London.
Renewed in U.S.A. 1978.

Photocopying this copyright material is **ILLEGAL**.

UNIS
mer - ry, let's sing and be mer - ry, be mer - ry with - al.
Pfte.
p
Here's
p
Let's
Ap - ril, here's May, here's June and Ju - ly, What plea - sure to see the corn
sing, sing, sing and be mer - ry with - al,
grow, In Au - gust we moil it, we reap, sheath and tie, And go
f
Let's sing, sing, sing and be mer - ry, be
down with our scythes, for to mow.
UNIS
mer - ry, let's sing and be mer - ry, be mer - ry with - al.
Pfte.

ff
Let's sing,
ff
And when we have la - boured and reaped ev - ery sheaf, And
let's sing, sing, sing,
glean - èd up ev - e - ry ear, We'll make no more a - do but to
sing and be mer - ry with - al Let's sing, sing,
plough we will go, To pro - vide for the ve - ry next year
sing and be mer - ry, be mer - ry, be mer - ry, be mer - ry, be mer - ry, Let's
ff
Let's
molto rit.
a tempo
sing and be mer - ry with - al.
Pfte.
molto rit.
a tempo
sing and be mer - ry with - al.
segue

I SPRING

1 EARLY IN THE SPRING

For Three Voices (unaccompanied)

Folk-song

Arranged by
R. VAUGHAN WILLIAMS

tak - ing of the air, O, They were tak - ing of the
lov - ers see, They were tak - ing of the air, O, They were
lov - ers see, They were tak - ing of the air, O, They were
air, O. Ah
tak - ing of the air, O. Ah
tak - ing of the air, O. Then this young cou - ple they walked a - long, And
Ah Think - ing to gain her fa - vour,
Ah Think - ing to gain her fa - vour, think -
this young man he sang a song, Think - ing to gain her fa - vour, think -
think - ing to gain her fa - vour. 'Since you have gained my
- ing, think - ing to gain her fa - vour. 'Since you've gained my
- ing to gain her fa - vour, her fa - vour. 'Since you've gained my
heart', said she 'And stolen a - way my li - ber - ty, Pray grant to me your
heart', said she 'And stolen a - way my li - ber - ty, Pray grant to me your
heart', said she 'And stolen a - way my li - ber - ty, Pray grant to me your

name, Sir, pray grant to me your name, Sir, grant me your
name, Sir, pray grant to me your name, Sir, To
name, Sir, pray grant to me your name, Sir, grant me your
p
name'. Ah Ah
church then this young cou - ple went, And mar - ried were, in sweet con - tent, She
p
name'. Ah Ah
f
Ah She and her own true
f
and her own true lov - - er, She and her own true lov - - er, own true
f
Ah She and her own true
lov - - - - er, She and her own true lov - - - - er.
lov - - - - er, She and her own true lov - - - - er.
lov - - - - - er, She and her own true lov - - - - er.

segue

2 THE LARK IN THE MORNING

(Two Voices with accompaniment)

Folk-song

Arranged by
R. VAUGHAN WILLIAMS

★NOTE: When this song is sung alone these seventeen bars should be omitted

p
And when the pret - ty plough - boy his day's work is
mf
And when the pret - ty plough - boy his day's work is
done, He trips down to the mea - - dows where the
done, He trips down to the mea - dows where the
grass the grass is all cut down, And there with his
f
grass is all cut down, And there with his
f
sweet - heart he'll dance and he'll sing, And at night
sweet - heart he'll dance and he'll sing, And at night
dim.
he will re - turn with his lass, At night he will re - turn with his
dim.
he will re - turn with his lass, At night he will re - turn with his
p
pp
lass home a - gain.
p
pp
lass home a - gain.
segue

3 MAY SONG

(For Full Chorus and Semi-chorus unaccompanied)

Folk-song

Arranged by
R. VAUGHAN WILLIAMS

ALL VOICES
f
Ah
The
fields they are so green, so green, So green, as an - y leaf; Our
Lord, our God has wa - tered them with heaven - ly dew so sweet.
Pfte.
DESCANT SOP. Semi-chorus
A -
FULL CHORUS only
Piano
A - wake, a - wake, you pret - ty, pret - ty maid, Out
- wake, a - wake, A -
of your ros - y dream, And step in - to your dai - ry be - low And
wake, you pret - ty, pret - ty, pret - ty, pret - ty
fetch us a bowl of cream.

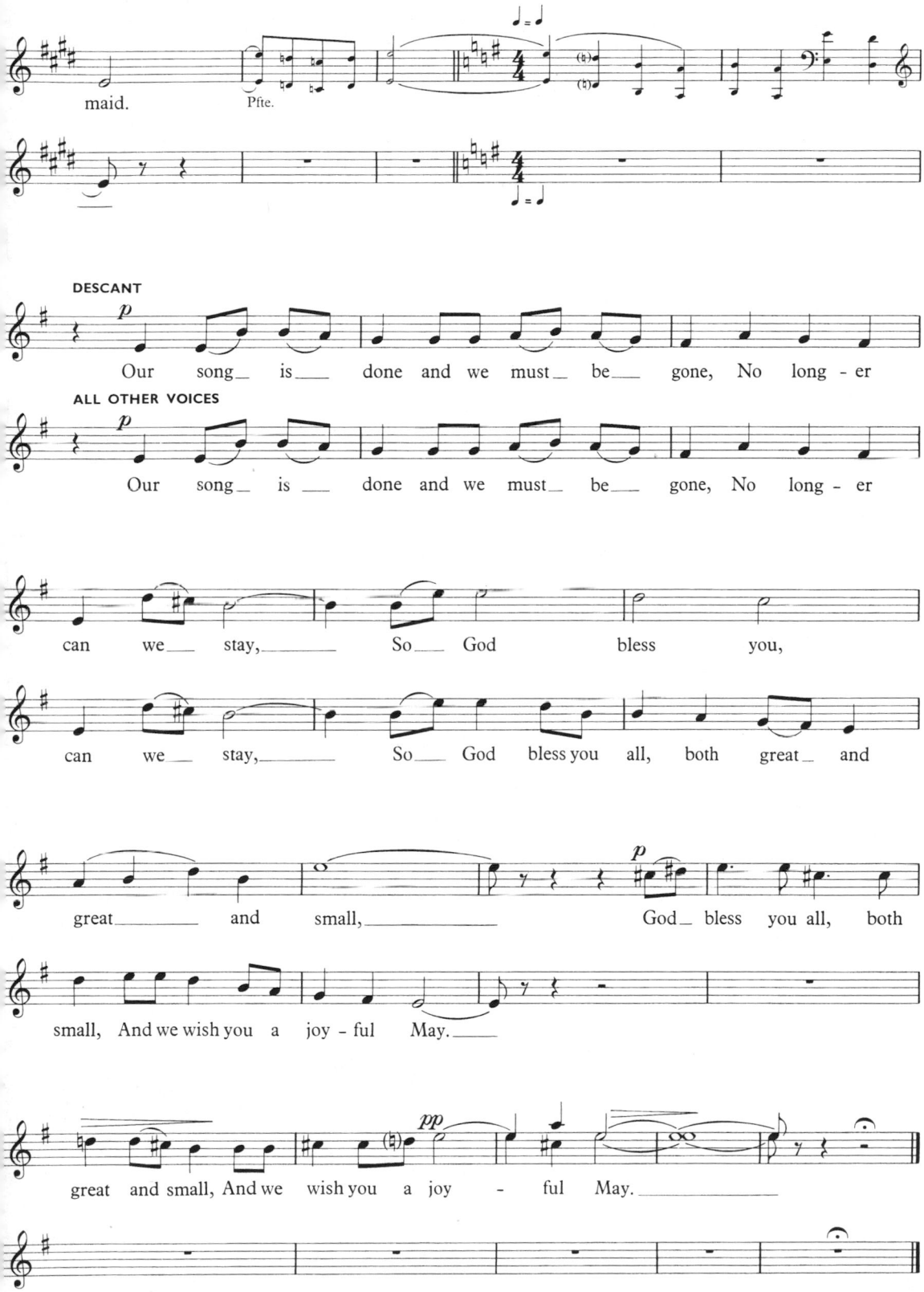
maid.
Pfte.
DESCANT
Our song is done and we must be gone, No long - er
ALL OTHER VOICES
Our song is done and we must be gone, No long - er
can we stay, So God bless you,
can we stay, So God bless you all, both great and
great and small, God bless you all, both
small, And we wish you a joy - ful May.
great and small, And we wish you a joy - ful May.

II SUMMER

1 SUMMER IS A-COMING IN and THE CUCKOO

(For Full Chorus and Semi-chorus, four parts)

Folk-song

Arranged by
R. VAUGHAN WILLIAMS

FULL CHORUS
p
Sum - mer is a - com - ing in,
cresc.
Grow - eth seed and blow - eth mead And spring'th the wood a - new.
Loud - ly sing cuc - koo,
cresc.
Grow - eth seed and blow - eth mead And
p
Sum - mer is a - com - ing in,
Loud - ly sing cuc - koo,
p
Sum - mer is a - com - ing in,
Loud - ly sing cuc - koo,
cresc.
Grow - eth seed and blow - eth mead And
f
Sing cuc - koo,
Mer - ry sing cuc -
spring'th the wood a - new.
f
Sing cuc - koo,
cresc.
Grow - eth seed and blow - eth mead And spring'th the wood a - new.
Loud - ly sing cuc - koo,
cresc.
Grow - eth seed and blow - eth mead And
spring'th the wood a - new.
f
Sing cuc - koo,
- koo, cuc - koo, cuc - koo, well sing - est thou cuc -
Mer - ry sing cuc - koo, cuc - koo,
f
Sing cuc - koo,
Mer - ry sing cuc -
spring'th the wood a - new.
f
Sing cuc - koo,

Mer - ry sing cuc - koo, Sing cuc - koo, sing cuc -
- koo, Sing cuc - koo, sing cuc - koo,
Cuc - koo well sing - est thou cuc - koo, Sing cuc - koo,
- koo, sing cuc - koo, Sing cuc - koo,
Mer - ry sing cuc - koo, Sing cuc - koo, sing cuc -
niente
- koo.
1st time to Andante sostenuto
2nd time Fine
p
sing cuc - koo.
niente
sing cuc - koo.
niente
sing cuc - koo.
1st time to Andante sostenuto
2nd time Fine
niente
koo.
Andante sostenuto ♩ = 94
Pfte.
8
SEMI-CHORUS
SOLO (or a FEW VOICES)
O the cuc - koo she's a
pret - ty bird, She sing - eth as she flies; She bring - eth good ti - dings, She

NOTE: The first of these melodies is an adaption of the famous 'Reading Rota' which though nominally composed by John of Forncete is undoubtedly a setting of a folk-tune.

2 THE SPRIG OF THYME

(Two Voices with accompaniment)

Folk-song

Arranged by
R. VAUGHAN WILLIAMS

NOTE: The arranger cannot trace the source of the above version of this well known melody, he hopes that no copyright has been infringed.

red, I gath-ered the rose so dear, I gained but the
soon; The li - ly and pink I ov - er-looked And vowed I would wait till
me; But when I gath-ered the rose so dear I gained but the wil - low
v.4 only
wil - - - - low tree,
June.
tree.
Pfte.
5. My gar - den is now run
wil - low it will
DESCANT Verse 6 only
Green wil - low will twist,
wild, When shall I plant it new? My bed that once was
twist, Green wil - low it will twine; And I wish I was in that
1
will twine, That
filled with thyme Is all ov - er - run with rue.
young mans arm's That once had the heart of mine.
6. Green
2
DESCANT
pp
once had the heart of mine.
FULL CHORUS
mine, The heart of mine.
Alternative for massed singing
mine.
segue

3 THE SHEEP SHEARING

For Two Voices unaccompanied

Folk-song

Arranged by
R. VAUGHAN WILLIAMS

lad takes his lass All on the green grass, And it's all
lad takes his lass All on the green grass, And it's all
to plough Where the fat ox - en graze low, And the lads and the
to plough Where the fat ox - en graze low, And the lads and the
lass - es to sheep-shear - ing go.
lass - es to sheep-shear - ing go.
p
When
pp
We'll pipe and we'll sing, love,
we have a - sheared all our jol - ly, jol - ly sheep, What joy can be
We'll dance in a ring, love, And it's
great - er than to talk of their in-crease? We'll pipe and we'll sing, love, We'll

all to plough, it's all
dance in a ring love, When each lad takes his lass All
to plough, all all to plough,
on the green grass, And it's all to plough
cresc.
And it's all to plough Where the
cresc.
Where the fat ox - en graze low, And the lads and the
f
p
fat ox - en graze low, And the lads and the lass - es to
f
p
lass - es to sheep shear - ing go, And it's all to
pp
sheep shear - ing go.
pp
plough where the ox - en graze low.
segue

4 THE GREEN MEADOW

Unison (All Voices)

Folk-song

Arranged by
R. VAUGHAN WILLIAMS

*This replaces a missing line in the original

III AUTUMN

1 JOHN BARLEYCORN

Full Chorus, (Unison) and Semi-chorus, (Two parts with accompaniment)

Folk-song

Arranged by
R. VAUGHAN WILLIAMS

Melody and some of the words from the collection of the late Cecil Sharp

SOPRANO Semi-chorus
2. A plough, an oath,
5. Came men They served,
took a plough and ploughed him in, Laid clods up - on his head: And
soon came men with their sharp scythes And chopped him to the knee, They
John Bar - ley-corn is
they served him bar bar-ous - -
they have tak-en a so - lemn oath John Bar - ley-corn is
rolled and tied him by the waist And served him bar-bar-ous-
dead, John Bar - ley-corn is dead.
- ly, they served him bar-bar-ous - ly.
ff
fol did-dle, did-dle,
dead.
- ly.
Sing Right fol did-dle, did-dle,
p
ff
Sing Right fol lol the did-dle al the dee,
Pfte.
right fol did-dle did-dle dee.
right fol did-dle did-dle dee.
right fol lee - ro dee.

f
3. So then he lay for three long weeks Till the dew from heaven did
6. We'll tip white wine in to a glass And scar - let in - to a
fall: John Bar - ley - corn sprang up a - gain
can, John Bar - ley - corn and his brown bowl
And that sur - prised them all. Did - dle did - dle dol,
Shall prove the bet - ter man. Did - dle did - dle dol,
ff
And that sur - prised them all. Sing did - dle did - dle dol,
Shall prove the bet - ter man. Sing did - dle did - dle dol,
p
ff
Sing Right fol lol the
did - dle, did - dle did - dle, did - dle dol the did - dle, right fol lee - ro
did - dle al the dee, right fol lee - ro
Pfte.
1
2
dee.
dee.
segue

2 THE UNQUIET GRAVE

(Three Voices unaccompanied)

Folk-song

Arranged by
R. VAUGHAN WILLIAMS

pp
cold
cold
my true love, And a few small drops of rain; I nev - er had but
pp
cold
cold
slain,
one true love And in green - wood he was slain. And in
cold
slain.
mf
slain,
I'll
mf
green wood he was slain,
I'll
mf
slain.
I'll
cantabile
do as much for my true love As an - y young girl may,
I'll
cantabile
do as much for my true love As an - y young girl may,
I'll
cantabile
do as much for my true love As an - y young girl may,
I'll

sit and weep down by his grave For twelve months and a day, for
sit and weep down by his grave For twelve months and a day, for
sit and weep down by his grave For twelve months and a day, for
p cantabile
twelve months and a day. But when twelve months were
pp
twelve months and a day.
pp
twelve months and a day.
pp
come and gone This young man he a - rose, weep
pp
a - rose, weep
p cantabile
a - rose, 'What makes you weep down
're - pose, re - pose, re -
're - pose, re - pose, re -
by my grave? I can't take my re - pose, I can't take my re -

pp
mp
- pose, re - pose.' 'One
- pose, re - pose.' 'One
- pose, re - pose.' 'One
poco agitato
kiss, one kiss of your li - ly white lips, One kiss is all I
kiss, one kiss of your li - ly white lips, One kiss is all I
kiss, One kiss I
f
crave, One kiss of your lips And re -
f
crave, One kiss, one kiss of your li - ly white lips, And re -
f
crave, One kiss, one kiss of your lips And re -
-turn back to your grave, And re - turn
-turn back to your grave, And re - turn back to your
- turn re - turn And re - turn

pp
back to your grave.' 'My lips
pp
grave.' 'My lips
pp
cantabile
back to your grave.' 'My lips they are as
are cold, are cold,
are cold, are cold,
cold as clay, My breath is earth-y and strong, If
pp
cold, long,
pp
cold, long,
you were to kiss my li - ly white lips, Your days would not be
your days would not be long,
your days would not be long,
long, your days would not be long, would

pp
p tranquillo
'My time be long, my time be short, To -
pp
p tranquillo
'My time be long, my time be short, To -
pp
p tranquillo
not be long, 'My time be long, my time be short, To -
f
- mor - row or to - day Sweet Christ in Heaven have all
f
- mor-row or to - day Sweet Christ in Heaven have all my soul And
f
- mor - row or to - day Sweet Christ in Heaven have all my soul And
p
my soul And take my life a -
p
take my life a - way, And take my life a - way.
p
take my life a - way, And take my life a - way.
morendo
niente
- way, a way.
morendo
niente
a - way, a - way, a - way.
morendo
niente
a - way, a - way, a - way.
segue

3 AN ACRE OF LAND

All Voices Unison

Folk-song

Arranged by
R. VAUGHAN WILLIAMS

IV WINTER

1 CHILDREN'S CHRISTMAS SONG

For Two Voices with accompaniment

Folk-song

Arranged by
R. VAUGHAN WILLIAMS

* When this song is sung alone start here

1
2
2. We Was - sail
was - sail Was
3. Good Mas - ter and good Mis - tress, While you're sit - ting by the
(4) purse Made of leath - ern rat - chin
- sail Was
fire, Pray think of us poor chil - dren that wan - der in the
skin We want a lit - tle of your mon - ey To line it well with -
- sail For it's Christ - mas time, when we tra - vel far and
mire.
- in. For it's Christ - mas time, when we tra - vel far and near; May God
near; May God bless you and send you a hap - py new year.
bless you and send you a hap - py new year.
Pfte.
1
Was
4. We've got a lit - tle

2
Piano
f
5. Bring us out a ta - ble, And
spread it with a cloth, Bring us out a mould - y cheese And
some of your Christ - mas loaf. For it's Christ - mas time, when we tra - vel far and
near; May God bless you and send you a hap - py new
year, May God send you a hap - - -
May God send you a hap - py, a
rall.
p
- - py, a hap - py new year.
hap - py new year.
segue

2 WASSAIL SONG

For All Voices with Descant

Folk-song

Arranged by
R. VAUGHAN WILLIAMS

2
DESCANT
f
Was - sail Was - sail Was - sail
FULL CHORUS
f
5. Come but - ler, come fill us a bowl of the best, Then I pray your
Was - sail
soul in heaven may rest, But if you do bring us a
Was - sail
bowl of the small, May the dev - il take but - ler, bowl and
p
Was - sail Was - sail Was - sail
p
all! 6. Then here's to the maid in the

Was - sail Was - sail
li - ly white smock, Who tripped to the door and slipped back the
cresc.
Was - sail Was - sail
cresc.
f
lock, Who tripped to the door and pulled back the pin, For to
f
Was - sail - - - - - - ers walk in Was - sail
let these jol - ly Was - sail - ers walk in
Who tripped to the door and pulled back the pin, For to
ff
Who tripped to the door and pulled back the pin, For to
rall.
a tempo
let these jol - ly Was - sail - ers walk in.
rall.
a tempo
let these jol - ly Was - sail - ers walk in.
segue

3 IN BETHLEHEM CITY

For Three Voices (unaccompanied)

Folk-song

Arranged by
R. VAUGHAN WILLIAMS

mer-ry, cast sor - row a - side, our Sav-iour Christ Jes-us was born on this tide.
mer-ry, cast sor - row a - side, our Sav - iour Christ Jes-us was born on this tide.
mer-ry, cast sor - row a - side, our Sav - iour Christ Jes-us was born on this tide.
p
2. But Ma - ry's full time be-ing come as we find, She brought forth her
4. Then God sent an an - gel from Hea - ven so high, To cer - tain poor
p
2. But Ma - ry's full time be-ing come as we find, She brought forth her
4. Then God sent an an - gel from Hea - ven so high, To cer - tain poor
p
2. But Ma - ry's full time be-ing come as we find, She brought forth her
4. Then God sent an an - gel from Hea - ven so high, To cer - tain poor
first born to save all man kind; The inn be - ing full, for the hea - ven - ly
shep-herds in fields where they lie, And bade them no long - er in sor - row to
first born to save all man kind; The inn be - ing full, for the hea - ven - ly
shep-herds in fields where they lie, And bade them no long - er in sor - row to
first born to save all man kind; The inn be - ing full, for the hea - ven - ly
shep-herds in fields where they lie, And bade them no long - er in sor - row to
pp f
guest No place could she find to lay Him to rest. Then
stay Be - cause that our Sav - iour was born on this day.
pp f
guest No place could she find to lay Him to rest. Then
stay Be - cause that our Sav - iour was born on this day.
pp f
guest No place could she find to lay Him to rest. Then
stay Be - cause that our Sav - iour was born on this day.

let us be mer - ry, cast sor - row a - side, Our Sav - iour Christ Je - sus was
let us be mer - ry, cast sor - row a - side, Our Sav - iour Christ Je - sus was
let us be mer - ry, cast sor - row a - side, Our Sav - iour Christ Je - sus was
pp
born on this tide. 3. Then they were con - strain - ed in a sta - ble to
5. Then pre - sent - ly af - ter the shep - herds did
pp
born on this tide. 3. Then they were con strain - ed in a sta - ble to
5. Then pre - sent - ly af - ter the shep - herds did
pp
born on this tide. 3. Then they were con - strain - ed in a sta - ble to
5. Then pre - sent - ly af - ter the shep - herds did
lie, Where hor - ses and as - ses they used for to tie. Their lodg - ing so
spy, Vast num - bers of an - gels did stand in the sky; So mer - ry were
lie, Where hor - ses and as - ses they used for to tie. Their lodg - ing so
spy, Vast num - bers of an - gels did stand in the sky; So mer - ry were
lie, Where hor - ses and as - ses they used for to tie. Their lodg - ing so
spy, Vast num - bers of an - gels did stand in the sky; So mer - ry were

cresc.
f
sim - ple they took in no scorn, Our Sav - - - iour, our Sav - iour was
talk - ing, so sweet - ly did sing, All glo - ry and praise to our
cresc.
f
sim - ple they took in no scorn, But a - gainst the next morn - ing our Sav - iour was
talk - ing, so sweet - ly did sing, All glo - ry and praise to our heaven - ly
cresc.
f
sim - ple they took in no scorn, But a - gainst the next morn - ing Our Sav - iour, was
talk - ing, so sweet - ly did sing, All glo - ry and praise to our heaven - ly
, ff
born.
hea - ven - ly King. Then let us be mer - ry, cast sor - row a - side, Our
, ff
born.
King. Then let us be mer - ry, cast sor - row a - side, Our
, ff
born.
heaven - ly King. Then let us be mer - ry, cast sor - row a - side, Our
rit.
1
2
Sav - iour Christ Jes - us was born on this tide. born on this tide.
Sav - iour Christ Jes - us was born on this tide. born on this tide.
Sav - iour Christ Jes - us was born on this tide. born on this tide.
segue

4 GOD BLESS THE MASTER

(From the 'Sussex Mummers' Carol')

For all Voices with Descant last verse

Folk-song

Arranged by
R. VAUGHAN WILLIAM

★ When this number is sung alone start here

OXFORD UNIVERSITY PRESS

Printed and bound in Great Britain by Caligraving Ltd, Thetford, Norfolk.

OXFORD
UNIVERSITY PRESS

www.oup.com

ISBN 978-0-19-387100-7